THE THOROUGHBRED HORSE

By Sara Green

Consultant:
Dr. Emily Leuthner
DVM, MS, DACVIM
Country View Veterinary Service
Oregon, Wisc.

BELLWETHER MEDIA • MINNEAPOLIS, MN

Jump into the cockpit and take flight with **Pilot Books**. Your journey will take you on high-energy adventures as you learn about all that is wild, weird, fascinating, and fun!

This edition first published in 2012 by Bellwether Media, Inc.

No part of this publication may be reproduced in whole or in part without written permission of the publisher. For information regarding permission, write to Bellwether Media, Inc., Attention: Permissions Department, 5357 Penn Avenue South, Minneapolis, MN 55419.

Library of Congress Cataloging-in-Publication Data

Green, Sara, 1964-
The Thoroughbred horse / by Sara Green.
   p. cm. – (Pilot books. Horse breed roundup)
Includes bibliographical references and index.
 Summary: "Engaging images accompany information about the Thoroughbred horse. The combination of high-interest subject matter and narrative text is intended for students in grades 3 through 7"–Provided by publisher.
 ISBN 978-1-60014-661-9 (hardcover : alk. paper)
 1. Thoroughbred horse–Juvenile literature. I. Title.
 SF293.T5G74 2011
 636.1'32–dc23   2011019680

Printed in the United States of America, North Mankato, MN.

080111   1187

CONTENTS

The Thoroughbred Horse

A bell rings and the starting gates swing open. Twenty Thoroughbreds burst out of the gates and charge down the track. Their hooves thunder as they **gallop** faster and faster. Suddenly, one horse breaks away from the rest. The crowd cheers as it crosses the finish line!

Thoroughbreds are among the fastest animals in the world. Some can run more than 40 miles (64 kilometers) per hour. Thoroughbreds are built to race. Their long, straight legs, sloped shoulders, and muscular **hindquarters** allow them to have longer **strides** than other horse breeds. Thoroughbreds have slim bodies with short, curved backs. They also have long, graceful necks and straight heads. Their eyes are large and wide-set. This physical build brings with it an energetic **temperament**. When you look into the eyes of the **hot-blooded** Thoroughbred, you can see its determined spirit.

Thoroughbreds are tall horses. They stand 15 to 17 **hands** high from the ground to the **withers**. This is between 60 and 68 inches (152 and 173 centimeters) tall. They weigh 900 to 1,200 pounds (410 to 540 kilograms).

Thoroughbred coats can be bay, brown, chestnut, black, gray, or **roan**. Bay horses are reddish brown with black manes and tails. Chestnuts are copper in color. Some Thoroughbreds are completely white, although this is rare. Many Thoroughbreds have white markings on their faces and legs, but few have white patterns on their bodies. No matter its color, every Thoroughbred runs down the track with style!

Springy Step

When a Thoroughbred runs, its back legs straighten out and act like springs. Its front legs pull it forward with tremendous power.

7

The Story of the Greatest Racehorse

The story of the Thoroughbred breed begins over 300 years ago in England. In the 1500s, horse racing became a popular sport there. The fastest horses at that time were Arabian horses. However, they were also small. Racing fans wanted a new breed that was faster and larger than the Arabians.

In the late 1600s and early 1700s, three Arabian **stallions** were brought to England from the **Middle East**. Their names were the Darley Arabian, the Byerly Turk, and the Godolphin Arabian. These stallions were bred with 74 **mares** that lived in England. The mares came from a variety of breeds, but they were all strong and tall. Their **foals** were the first Thoroughbreds. Today, all Thoroughbreds can trace their **pedigrees** to those three Arabian stallions.

What's in a Name?

The Jockey Club has strict rules for naming Thoroughbred foals. Names cannot be longer than 18 letters, contain initials, or end with numbers. Owners also cannot give their foals the same names as well-known horses.

In 1730, the first Thoroughbred was brought to the American colonies. He was a stallion named Bulle Rock, and his father was the Darley Arabian. Throughout the rest of the 1700s and into the 1800s, the popularity of the breed grew rapidly in the United States. As American **settlers** began to move west, they took their Thoroughbreds with them. Many Thoroughbred owners settled in Tennessee and Kentucky. By the 1820s, Kentucky had many racetracks. The state became famous for Thoroughbred breeding and racing.

As more people began owning Thoroughbreds, owners decided to keep records of the breed. They formed The Jockey Club in 1894. This organization keeps track of the names and pedigrees of all Thoroughbreds born in North America. Today, The Jockey Club **registers** almost 30,000 foals every year.

Racing, Sports, and Trail Riding

Thoroughbreds begin training for races when they are 18 months old. In Thoroughbred races, **jockeys** ride horses at top speeds around a flat, oval track. Thoroughbred races range from five-eighths of a mile to 1.5 miles (1 to 2.4 kilometers). A Thoroughbred's single stride can cover more than 20 feet (6 meters) of ground!

Thoroughbred racing is popular all over the world. People enjoy attending races and picking which horses they think will come in first, second, and third place. Winning horses get awards after a race. In the Breeders' Cup World Championship race, the horse that comes in first place receives a trophy and a blanket made of flowers to wear on its withers.

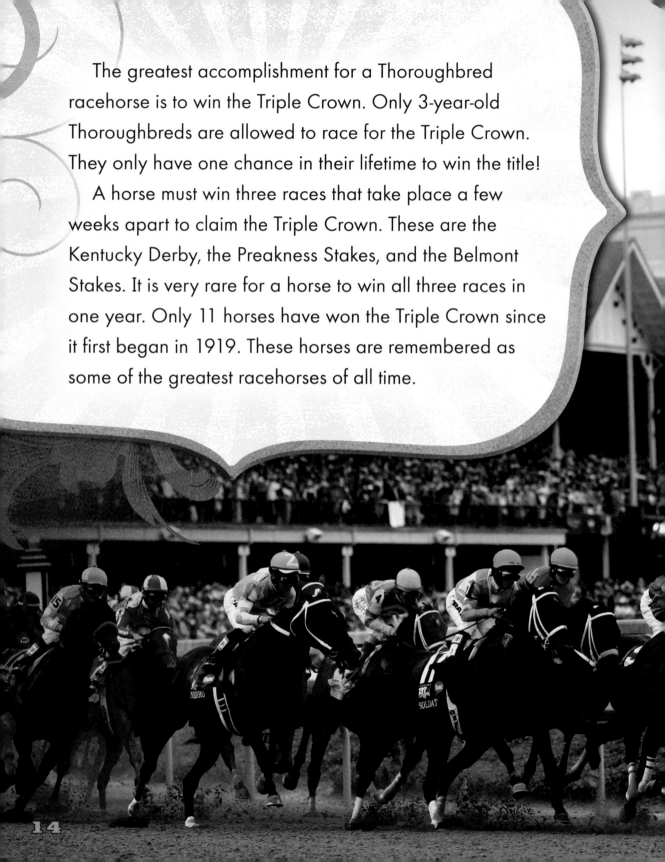

The greatest accomplishment for a Thoroughbred racehorse is to win the Triple Crown. Only 3-year-old Thoroughbreds are allowed to race for the Triple Crown. They only have one chance in their lifetime to win the title!

A horse must win three races that take place a few weeks apart to claim the Triple Crown. These are the Kentucky Derby, the Preakness Stakes, and the Belmont Stakes. It is very rare for a horse to win all three races in one year. Only 11 horses have won the Triple Crown since it first began in 1919. These horses are remembered as some of the greatest racehorses of all time.

Triple Crown Winners

Sir Barton (1919)
Gallant Fox (1930)
Omaha (1935)
War Admiral (1937)
Whirlaway (1941)
Count Fleet (1943)
Assault (1946)
Citation (1948)
Secretariat (1973)
Seattle Slew (1977)
Affirmed (1978)

Kentucky Derby

The Thoroughbred's speed helps it compete in sports other than racing. In polo, teams of four riders try to score goals against each other. Riders use long-handled mallets to hit a small ball. Horses that participate in polo are traditionally called "polo ponies," even though they are full-sized horses. Many of the best polo ponies are Thoroughbreds. With their speed and **agility**, Thoroughbreds can accelerate and change direction quickly to get their riders to the ball.

A Tall Order
In high-jump competitions, the last wall horses must jump over is often more than 7 feet (2 meters) high!

The Thoroughbred's height gives it an advantage in show jumping. In this sport, riders guide horses to jump over fences, poles, walls, water, and other obstacles. Teams lose points if they touch or knock over obstacles. The team with the most points wins the competition. Show jumping has become such a popular sport that it is now part of the **Olympics**.

Famous Thoroughbreds

Eclipse

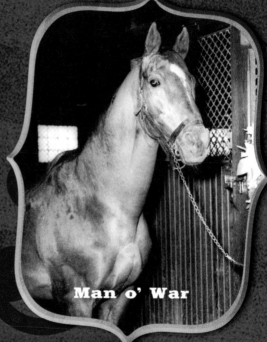

Man o' War

Eclipse

In 1769, the fastest Thoroughbred was a chestnut stallion named Eclipse. He was the great-great-grandson of the Darley Arabian. Eclipse raced for one and a half years and never lost. He fathered hundreds of foals. Today, more than 3 out of every 4 registered Thoroughbreds can trace their pedigrees to Eclipse.

Man o' War

Many racing experts believe Man o' War was the greatest racehorse that ever lived. This chestnut Thoroughbred was born in 1917. He had a stride that was 28 feet (8.5 meters) long. In two years of racing, Man o' War won 20 of his 21 races. His son War Admiral won the Triple Crown in 1937.

Seabiscuit

Secretariat

Seabiscuit

Seabiscuit was a small Thoroughbred with crooked legs that became a racing hero. In 1938, he defeated Triple Crown winner War Admiral in a one-on-one race. People called this the "Match of the Century," and War Admiral had been the clear favorite. For this win and others, Seabiscuit was named Horse of the Year. He received more news coverage that year than any other public figure in the world!

Secretariat

Secretariat became a racing legend when he won the Triple Crown in 1973. Secretariat set new records in the Kentucky Derby and the Belmont Stakes. To this day, no horse has broken these records. After retiring from racing, Secretariat fathered 653 foals, 57 of which became champion racehorses.

Thoroughbreds will always be known for their incredible speed and **endurance**. Although many stop racing at younger ages, Thoroughbreds are allowed to race until they turn 15 years old. Even after they are too old to race, Thoroughbreds enjoy staying active. Many retired racehorses become trail horses. These Thoroughbreds are often called Off-the-Track-Thoroughbreds, or OTTBs. They are more relaxed and easier to ride than younger, more energetic Thoroughbreds.

Whether they are racing, playing polo, or walking on trails, Thoroughbreds enjoy spending time with people. They are extremely loyal to their riders and develop deep bonds with their trainers. People can't help but love Thoroughbreds for their friendly temperament and spirit off the track. On the track, none can compete against the fierce Thoroughbred, the greatest racehorse in the world!

Glossary

agility—the ability to move the body quickly and with ease

endurance—the ability to do something for a long time

foals—young horses; foals are under one year old.

gallop—the fastest gait of a horse; a gallop averages 25 to 30 miles (40 to 48 kilometers) per hour.

hands—the units used to measure the height of a horse; one hand is equal to 4 inches (10.2 centimeters).

hindquarters—the hind legs and muscles of a four-legged animal

hot-blooded—energetic and tough; hot-blooded horses have a lot of speed and endurance.

jockeys—people who ride racehorses

mares—adult female horses

Middle East—an area of southwest Asia and northeast Africa that stretches from the Mediterranean Sea to Pakistan

Olympics—international games held every two years; the Olympics alternate between summer sports and winter sports.

pedigrees—records or lists of ancestors

registers—makes record of; owners register their horses with official breed organizations.

roan—a coat with a dark base color and white hairs

settlers—people who come to live in a new land

stallions—adult male horses that are used for breeding

strides—distances between footsteps

temperament—personality or nature; the Thoroughbred has a spirited, energetic temperament.

withers—the ridge between the shoulders of a horse

To Learn More

At the Library

Campbell, Joanna. *A Horse Called Wonder.* New York, N.Y.: HarperPaperbacks, 1991.

Rumsch, BreAnn. *Thoroughbred Horses.* Edina, Minn.: ABDO Pub. Co., 2011.

Stone, Lynn M. *Thoroughbred Horses.* Vero Beach, Fla.: Rourke Pub., 2008.

On the Web

Learning more about Thoroughbreds is as easy as 1, 2, 3.

1. Go to www.factsurfer.com.

2. Enter "Thoroughbreds" into the search box.

3. Click the "Surf" button and you will see a list of related Web sites.

With factsurfer.com, finding more information is just a click away.

Index

The images in this book are reproduced through the courtesy of: PICANI / imagebroker / Age Fotostock, front cover, pp. 8-9; Cheryl Ann Quigley, pp. 4-5, 12-13; Juniors Bildarchiv / Photolibrary, pp. 6-7; National Geographic Image Collection / Alamy, pp. 10-11; AFP / Getty Images, pp. 14-15; Heinz Kühbauch / Photolibrary, p. 16; Tim Graham / Getty Images, p. 17; Mary Evans Picture Library / Alamy, p. 18 (left); Associated Press, p. 18 (right); Sports Illustrated / Getty Images, p. 19 (left); Getty Images, p. 19 (right); Ellwood Eppard, pp. 20-21.